Lev Tolstoy

The Two Old Men

Lev Tolstoy

The Two Old Men

ISBN/EAN: 9783337330682

Printed in Europe, USA, Canada, Australia, Japan

Cover: Foto ©Thomas Meinert / pixelio.de

More available books at **www.hansebooks.com**

The Two Old Men

Lev Tolstoy

The Two Old Men by Lev Tolstoy

John IV. 19 - "The woman said unto him, Sir, I see that you are a prophet.

20. Our fathers worshipped in this mountain; and you say that in Jerusalem is the place where men ought to worship.

21. Jesus said unto her, woman, believe me, the hour cometh when ye shall neither in this mountain nor yet at Jerusalem worship the Father.

22. You worship you know not what: we know what we worship: for salvation is of the Jews.

23. But the hour comes, and now is, when the true worshippers shall worship the Father in spirit and in truth: for the Father seeks such to worship Him."

I

Two old men took it into their heads to go and pray to God in ancient Jerusalem. One of them was a rich peasant named Efim Tarassitch Sheveloff, and the other was a poor man named Elijah Bodroff.

Efim was a sober man. He drank no vodka, smoked no tobacco, sniffed no tobacco, had never breathed an oath in his life, and was altogether a strict and conscientious citizen. Twice he had served a term as administrator, and left office without a figure wrong in his books. He had a large family (his two sons, as well as a grandson, were married), and they all lived together. In person he was an upright, vigorous man, with a beard only begun to be streaked with grey now that he had attained his seventieth year.

Old Elijah, on the other hand, was a man neither rich nor poor, who, formerly a travelling carpenter, had now settled down and taken to bee-keeping. One of his sons earned his living at home, and the other one away. He was a good-hearted, cheerful old fellow, and drank vodka, smoked tobacco, sniffed tobacco, and loved a good song. None the less, he was of peaceable disposition, and lived on excellent terms both with his household and the neighbours. In himself he was a man of medium height, with a swarthy complexion and curly beard. Moreover, like his holy namesake, the Prophet Elijah, he was bald.

The two old men had long ago agreed to go upon this pilgrimage together, yet Efim had never been able to find time from his business. As soon as he had got one thing out of hand he would find himself hatching a new scheme. Now he would be marrying a granddaughter, now expecting his younger son home from military service, now planning to erect a new hut.

One day the old men met at a festival, and seated themselves together on a bench.

- Well, - said Elijah, - when are we going to carry out that long-agreed-upon scheme of ours?

Efim frowned.

- We must wait a little yet, - he said. - This last year has been a heard one for me. When I planned to build that new hut I reckoned it would cost me about a hundred roubles only, but already the estimate is rising up to three times that amount, and it hasn't come in yet. I must certainly wait until the summer. Then, if God pleases, we will go.

- Well, - replied Elijah, - it seems to me that we ought not to put it off any longer, but to go now. Spring is the very time for it.

- Time or no time, the work is begun now. How can I go and leave it?

- But have you no one to leave in charge? Surely your son could see to it?

- He indeed! Why, that eldest son of mine is perfectly useless. He would spoil it all.

- No, no, my old friend. Even if you and I died to-morrow, the world would still go on without us. Your son only needs a little teaching.

- That may be; yet I want to see the work finished under my own eyes.

- Pooh, my dear sir! One never really gets to the end of things. Why, only the other day our women at home were washing the linen and getting ready for the festival—first one thing having to be done, and then another, as if there would never be an end to it all—when at last my eldest daughter-in-law (and she is a clever woman) exclaimed: 'Never mind if the festival is coming on and we shan't be ready. However much we do, we can't do everything.'

Efim reflected a moment—then said:

- I have laid out a lot of money already on this building scheme, and it would hardly do to set forth on a journey with empty hands. A hundred roubles is no light sum to raise, you know.

Elijah smiled.

- Yes, you must be careful, - he said. - Why, your income is ten times as much as mine, yet you worry far more about money than I do. Look at me. Merely tell me when to start, and, little though I possess, I shall be there.

Efim smiled in his turn.

- Are you such a rich man, then, after all? – He said. - Where is it all going to come from?

- Oh, I shall scrape it together somehow—raise it somehow. If there is no other way of doing so, I shall sell a dozen of my range of bee-hives to a neighbour. He has long been after them.

- And then the swarms will turn out well, and you will be sorry for it.

- Sorry for it? No, no. I have never been sorry for anything in my life except for my sins. There is nothing worth troubling about except one's soul.

- That may be; yet it is awkward to have things go wrong at home.

- But it is still more awkward to have things go wrong with one's soul. Come now! You have as good as promised me, so we must really go. It would be only right of us to do so.

II

Thus Elijah won over his comrade. Next morning Efim took counsel with himself, and then went to see Elijah.

- Yes, we will go very soon now, - he said. – You were quite right. In life or in death we are in God's hands. We ought to go while we are still alive and well.

A week later the two got themselves ready. Efim always kept his money at home, and of it he took 190 roubles for the journey, and left 200 for the old woman. Elijah likewise made his preparations. He sold the neighbour ten out of his range of bee-hives, together with whatever stock of honey they might produce. That brought him in seventy roubles. Another thirty he swept together from one corner and another. His wife gave up the whole of her funeral savings, and their daughter-in-law did the same.

Efim confided the entire direction of his affairs at home to his eldest son, telling him which crops to pull while he was away, and how much of them, where to spread the manure, and how to build and roof the new hut. He thought of everything, left directions for everything. Elijah, on the other hand, merely told his old wife to be careful to collect such young bees as might leave the hives which he had disposed of, and deliver full tale of them to the neighbour. On other domestic matters he said not a word. Circumstances themselves would show what was to be done, and how it was to be done, as circumstances arose. Housewives, he thought, know their own business best.

So the two old men made them ready for the journey. Home-made cakes were baked, wallets contrived, new leggings cut out, new boots procured, and spare shoes provided. Then they set off. Their relatives escorted them to the end of the village, and there took leave of them. Thus the old men were fairly launched upon their way.

Elijah walked along in high spirits, and forgot all his domestic concerns immediately he had left the village. His only cares were how to please his companion during the way, to avoid uttering a rude word, and to arrive at his destination and return home in peace and love. As he walked along he whispered to himself a silent prayer, or thought of the lives of the saints, so far as he could remember.

Whether he came across anyone on the road, or turned in anywhere for the night, with each he endeavoured to associate amicably and with a pious word. As he went he rejoiced in heart. One thing, however, he could not do. He had resolved to leave off tobacco, and to that end had left his pipe at home—and he missed it sadly. On the way a man gave him one. Thereafter, lest he should cause his fellow-traveller to stumble, he would fall behind him and smoke quietly.

As for Efim, he walked circumspectly, determined to do nothing amiss and speak no light word, since frivolity was foreign to his soul. Likewise, his domestic cares never left his thoughts. He was forever thinking of how things might be going at home and of the directions he had given to his son, as well as wondering if those directions were being carried out. Whenever he saw peasants setting potatoes or carting manure he at once thought to himself: "Is my son doing as I instructed him?" Sometimes, indeed, he felt like turning back to give fresh directions and see them carried out in person.

III

When the old men had been on the tramp five weeks, their home-made bast shoes gave out, and they had to buy new ones. In time they arrived at Ukraine, where, although by this time they were far from the district where they were known and had for some time past been accustomed to pay for their board and lodging each night, these good people vied with each other in entertaining them. They took them in and fed them, yet would accept no money, but sped them on their way with food in their wallets and sometimes new bast shoes as well. Thus the old men covered 700 kilometers with ease, until they had crossed another province and arrived in bare and poverty-stricken land. Here still the inhabitants were willing to take them in, and would accept no money for their night's lodging, yet ceased to provide them with food. Nowhere was even bread given to the travellers, and occasionally it could not be bought. Last year, the people said, nothing had grown. Those who had been rich had ploughed up their land and sold out; those who had been only moderately rich were now reduced to nothing; while those who had been poor had either perished outright or emigrated, with the exception of a few, who still eked out a wretched existence somehow. During the past winter, indeed, such people had lived on chaff and weeds.

One evening the old men stayed the night at a place, and, having bought fifteen pounds of bread, went on before dawn, so as to get as far as possible while it was yet cool. They covered ten kilometers, and then sat down by a brook, ladled some water into a bowl, soaked and ate some bread, and washed their feet. As they sat and rested Elijah pulled out his horn tobacco-box, whereupon Efim shook his head in disapproval.

- Why not throw that rubbish away? - He said.

- Nay, but if a failing has got the better of one, what's one to do? - replied Elijah with a shrug of his shoulders.

Then they got up and went on for another ten kilometers. The day had now become intensely hot, and after reaching and passing through a large village,

Elijah grew weary, and longed to rest again and have a drink. Efim, however, refused to stop, for he was the better walker of the two, and Elijah often found it difficult to keep up with him.

- Oh, for a drink! - said Elijah.

- Well go and have one. I myself can do without.

Elijah stopped. - Do not wait for me, - he said. - I will run to that hut there and beg a drink, and be after you again in a twinkling."

- Very well, - said Efim, and he went on along the road alone, while Elijah turned aside to the hut.

When he came to it he saw that it was a small, plastered cabin, with its lower part black and the upper part white. The plaster was peeling off in patches, and had evidently not been renewed for many a long day, while in one side of the roof there was a large hole. The way to the hut door lay through a yard, and when Elijah entered the latter he saw a man — thin, clean-shaven, and clad only in a shirt and breeches, after the fashion of the Ukrainians - lying stretched beside a trench. Somehow he looked as though he were lying there for coolness' sake, yet the sun was glaring down upon him. There he lay, but not as though asleep. Elijah hailed him and asked for a drink, but the man returned no answer. "He must be either ill or uncivil," thought Elijah, and went on to the door of the hut, within which he could hear the voices of two children crying. He knocked first with the iron ring of the door-knocker, and called out "Mistress!" No one answered. Again he knocked with his pilgrim's staff and called out, "Good Christians!" Nothing stirred within the hut. "Servants of God!" He cried once more, and once more received no response. He was just on the point of turning to depart when he heard from behind the door a sound as of someone gasping. Had some misfortune come upon these people? He felt that he must find out, and stepped inside.

IV

Elijah turned the ring; the door was unlocked, and the handle turned easily.
Passing through a little entrance-porch, the inner door of which stood open,
Elijah saw on the left a stove, and in front of him the living portion of the
room. In one corner stood an ikon frame and a table, while behind the table
stood a wooden bench. Upon this bench was seated an old woman – bare-
headed, and wearing only a single garment. Her head was bowed upon her
arms, while beside her stood a little boy—thin, waxen in the face, and pot-
bellied—who kept clutching her by the sleeve and crying loudly as he
besought her for something. The air in the hut was stifling to the last degree.
Elijah stepped forward and caught sight of a second woman stretched on a
shelf-bunk behind the stove. She was lying face downwards, with her eyes
closed, but moaned at intervals as she threw out one of her legs and drew it
back again with a writhing movement. An oppressive odour came from the
bunk, and it was clear that she had no one to attend to her. All at once the old
woman raised her head and caught sight of the stranger.

- What do you want? - She asked in the Ukrainian dialect. - What do you
want? Nay, my good man, we have nothing for you here.

None the less, Elijah understood her dialect, and took a step nearer.

- I am a servant of God, - he said, - who crave of you a drink of water.

- Nay, but there is no one to get it for you, - she replied. - You must take what
you require and go.

- And is there no one well enough to wait upon this poor woman? - went on
Elijah, presently.

- No, no one. Her man is dying in the yard yonder, and there are only
ourselves besides.

The little boy had been stricken to silence by the entry of a stranger, but now the old woman had no sooner finished speaking than he clutched her again by the sleeve.

- Some bread, some bread, granny! - He cried, and burst out weeping.

Elijah was about to question the old woman further when a peasant staggered into the hut, supporting himself by the wall as he did so, and tried to sit down upon the bench. Missing his footing in the attempt, he rolled backwards upon the floor. He made no attempt to rise, but struggled to say something, speaking a word only at a time, with rests between each one.

- We have sickness here, - he gasped, - and famine too. That little one there, - and he nodded towards the boy, - is dying of hunger. He burst into tears.

Elijah unslung his wallet from his shoulders, freed his arms from the strap, and lowered the wallet to the floor. Then he lifted it, placed it on the bench, unfastened it, and, taking out some bread and a knife, cut off a hunch and held it out towards the peasant. Instead of taking it, the man made a movement of his head in the direction of the two children (there was a little girl there also, behind the stove), as much as to say, "Nay, give it to them." Accordingly Elijah handed the piece to the little boy, who no sooner caught sight of it than he darted forward, seized it in his tiny hands, and ran off, with his nose fairly buried in the crumb. At the same moment the little girl came out from behind the stove, and simply glued her eyes upon the bread. To her too Elijah handed a piece, and then cut off another for the old woman, who took it and began to chew it at once.

- I beseech you, get us some water, - she said presently.

- Our mouths are parched. I tried to draw some water this morning (or this afternoon—I hardly know which), but fell down under its weight. The bucket will be there now if you could only bring it.

Upon Elijah asking where the well was, the old woman told him, and he went off. He found the bucket there as she had described, brought some water, and gave each of them a drink. Now that they had had the water, the children managed to devour a second hunch apiece, and the old woman too, but the peasant would not touch anything. "I do not feel inclined," he said. As for his wife, she lay tossing herself to and fro on the bunk, unconscious of what was passing. Elijah returned to a shop in the village, bought some millet, salt, meal, and butter, and hunted out a hatchet. Then, having cut some firewood, he lighted the stove with the little girl's help, cooked some soup and porridge, and gave these poor people a meal.

V

The peasant ate but little, but the old woman did better, while the two children cleared a bowlful apiece, and then went to sleep in one another's arms. Presently the man and the old woman began telling Elijah how it had all come upon them.

- We used to make a living, - they said, - poor though it was; but when the crop failed last year we found we had exhausted our stock by the autumn, and had to eat anything and everything we could get. Then we tried to beg of neighbours and kind-hearted folk. At first they gave, but later they began to refuse us. There were many who would have given, but they had nothing to give. In time, too, it began to hurt us to beg, for we were in debt to everyone — in debt for money, meal, and bread.

- I tried to get work, - went on the peasant, - but there was almost none to be got. Everywhere there were starving men struggling for work. A man might get a little job one day, and then spend the next two in looking for another. The old woman and the little girl walked many a long distance for alms, though what they received was little enough, seeing that many, like ourselves, had not even bread. Still, we managed to feed ourselves somehow, and hoped to win through to the next season. But by the time spring came people had ceased to give at all, and sickness came upon us, and things grew desperate. One day we might have a bite of something to eat, and then nothing at all for two more. At last we took even to eating grass; and whether that was the cause or something else, the wife fell ill as you see. There she lay on the bed, while I myself had come to the end of my strength, and had no means of reviving it.

- Yes, I was the only one who held up, - went on the old woman, - Yet hunger was pulling me down as well, and I was getting weaker every day. The little girl was in the same plight as I was, and taking to having nervous fits. One day I wanted to send her to a neighbour's, but she would not go. She just crept behind the stove and refused. The day before yesterday another neighbour came and looked in; but as soon as she saw that we were ill and starving she turned round and went away again. You see, her own husband had just died, and she had nothing to give her little children to eat. So, when you came, we were just lying here—waiting for death to come.

Elijah listened to their tale, and decided that, as it was doubtful whether he could overtake Efim that day, he had better spend the night here. The next morning he rose and did the housework, as if he himself were the master. Then he helped the old woman to make dough, and lighted the stove. After that he accompanied the little girl to some neighbours' huts, to try and borrow what else was needed, but was unsuccessful everywhere. No one had anything at all—everything had been disposed of for food, down to household necessaries and even clothes. Consequently Elijah had to provide what was needed himself— to buy some things and make others. He spent the whole day like this, and then the next, and then a third. The little boy recovered himself, and began to walk along the bench and to frisk about Elijah, while the little girl grew quite merry and helped in everything. She was forever running after Elijah with her "Granddad! Granddaddy!" The old woman likewise picked up again, and went out to see a neighbour or two, while as for the husband, he progressed so far as to walk a little with the help of the wall. Only his wife still lay sick. Yet on the third day she too opened her eyes and asked for food.

"Now," - thought Elijah to himself, - "I must be off. I had not expected to be detained so long."

VI

It chanced, however, that the fourth (the next) day would be the first of the breaking the fast, or days of flesh-eating, and Elijah thought to himself: "How would it be if I were to break my fast with these people, buy them some presents for the festival, and then go on my way in the evening?" So he went to the village again, and bought milk, white meal, and lard. Everyone, from the old woman downwards, boiled and baked that day, and next morning Elijah went to Mass, returned to the hut, and broke his fast with his new friends. That day, too, the wife got up from her bed, and walked about a little. As for the husband, he shaved himself, put on a clean shirt (hastily washed for him by the old woman, since he had only one), and went off to the village to beg the forbearance of a rich peasant to whom both corn- and pasture-land had been mortgaged, and to pray that he would surrender them before the harvest. Towards evening the husband returned with a dejected air, and burst into tears. The rich peasant, it seemed, had refused his request, saying, "Bring me the money first."

Elijah took counsel with himself again. "How are these people to five without land." he thought. "Strangers will come and reap the crops, and leave nothing at all for them, since the crops are mortgaged. However good the rye may turn out to be (and Mother Earth is looking well now), strangers will come and harvest it all, and these people can look to receive nothing, seeing that their three acres of corn-land is in fee to the rich peasant. If I were to go away now, they would come to rack and ruin again.

He was so distressed by these thoughts that he did not leave that evening, but deferred his departure until the next morning. He went to sleep in the yard as usual, and lay down after he had said his prayers. Nevertheless his eyes would not close. "Yes, I ought to go," - he thought, - "for I have spent too much time and money here already. I am sorry for these people, but one cannot benefit everyone. I meant only to give them a drop of water and a slice of bread; yet see what that slice has led to! Still," - he went on, - "why not redeem their corn- and meadow-land while I am about it? Yes, and buy a cow for the children and a horse for the father's harvesting? Ah, well, you have got your ideas into a fine tangle, Elijah Kuzmitch! You are dragging your anchors, and can't make head or tail of things."

So he raised himself, took his cloak from under his head, turned it over until he had found his horn tobacco-box, and smoked to see if that would clear his thoughts. He pondered and pondered, yet could come to no decision. He wanted to go, and at the same time felt sorry for these people. Which way was it to be? He really did not know. At last he refolded his cloak under his head and stretched himself out again. He lay like that until the cocks were crowing, and then dozed off to sleep. Suddenly someone seemed to have aroused him, and he found himself fully dressed and girded with wallet and staff—found himself walking out of the entrance-gates of the yard. But those gates were so narrow, somehow, that even a single person could hardly get through them. First his wallet caught on one of the gates, and when he tried to release it, the gate on the other side caught his legging and tore it right open. Turning to release it also, he found that, after all, it was not the gate that was holding it, but the little girl, and that she was crying out, "Granddad! Granddaddy! Give me some bread!" Then he looked at his leg again, and there was the little boy also holding on to the legging, while their father and the old woman were looking from a window. He awoke, and said to himself: "I will buy out their land for them to-morrow - yes, and buy them a horse and cow as well. Of what avail is it to go across the sea to seek Christ if all the time I lose the Christ that is within me here? Yes, I must put these people straight again." - And he fell asleep until morning. He rose betimes, went to the rich peasant, and redeemed both the rye-crop and the hay. Then he went and bought a scythe (for these people's own scythe had been sold, together with everything else), and took it home with him. He set a man to mow the hay, while he himself went hunting among the men until he found a horse and cart for sale at the innkeeper's. He duly bargained for and bought it, and then continued his way in search of a cow. As he was walking along the street he overtook two Ukrainian women, who were chatting volubly to each other as they went. He could hear that it was of himself they were speaking, for one of the women said:

- When he first came they could not tell at all what he was, but supposed him to be a pilgrim. He only came to beg a drink of water, yet he has been there ever since. There is nothing he is not ready to buy them. I myself saw him buying a horse and cart today at the innkeeper's. There cannot be many such people in the world. I should like to see this marvellous pilgrim.

When Elijah heard this, and understood that it was himself they were praising, he forbore to go and buy the cow, but returned to the innkeeper and paid over the money for the horse and cart. Then he harnessed the horse, and drove home to the hut. Driving right up to the gates, he stopped and alighted. His hosts were surprised to see the horse, and although it crossed their minds that possibly he might have bought it for themselves, they hesitated to say so. However, the husband remarked as he ran to open the gates:

- So you have bought a new horse, then, grandfather?

To this Elijah merely answered:

- Yes, but I only bought it because it happened to be going cheap. Cut some fodder, will you, and lay it in the manger for its food to-night?

So the peasant unharnessed the horse, cut some swathes of grass, and filled the manger. Then everyone lay down to rest. But Elijah lay out upon the roadway, whither he had taken his wallet beforehand; and when all the people were asleep he arose, girded on his wallet, put on his boots and cloak, and went on his way to overtake Efim.

VII

When Elijah had gone about five kilometers, the day began to break. He sat down under a tree, opened his wallet, and began to make calculations. According to his reckoning, he had seventeen roubles and twenty kopeks left. "Well," he thought, "I can't get across the sea on that, and to raise the rest in Christ's name would be a sin indeed. Friend Efim must finish the journey alone, and offer my candle for me. Yes, my vow must remain unfulfilled now until I die; but, thanks be to God, the Master is merciful and longsuffering."

So he rose, slung his wallet across his shoulders, and went back. Yet he made a circuit of the village — of that village—so that the people should not see him. Soon he was near home again. When he had been travelling away from home, walking had been an effort, and he had hardly been able to keep up with Efim; but now that he was travelling towards home it seemed as if God helped his steps and never let him know weariness. As he went along he jested, swung his staff about, and covered seventy kilometers a day.

So he came home. A crowd gathered from the fields, far and near, and his entire household ran to greet their old head. Then they began to ply him with questions—as to how, when, and where everything had happened, why he had left his comrade behind, why l:e had returned home without completing the journey, and so on. Elijah did not make a long story of it.

- God did not see fit to bring me to my goal, - he said. - I lost some money on the road, and got separated from my companion. So I went no further. Pardon me, for Christ's sake, - and he handed what was left of the money to his old goodwife. Then he asked her about his domestic affairs. All was well with them, everything had been done, there had been no neglect of household management, and the family had lived in peace and amity.

Efim's people heard the same day that Elijah had returned, and went to him to ask about their own old man. Elijah merely told them the same story.

- Your old man, - he said, - was quite well when he parted from me. That was three days before the Feast of Saint Peter. I meant to catch him up later, but various matters intervened where I was. I lost my money, and had not enough to continue upon, so I came back.

Everyone was surprised that a man of such sense could have been so foolish as to set out and yet never reach his journey's end, but only waste his money. They were surprised—and then forgot all about it. Elijah did the same. He resumed his household work—helping his son to get firewood ready against the winter, giving the women a hand with the corn grinding, roofing the stable, and seeing to his bees. Likewise he sold another ten hives, with their produce, to the neighbour. His old wife wanted to conceal how many of the hives had been swarmed from, but Elijah knew without her telling him which of them had swarmed and which were barren, and handed over seventeen hives to the neighbour instead of ten. Then he put everything straight, sent off his son to look for work for himself, and sat down for the winter to plait bast shoes and carve wooden clogs.

VIII

All that day when Elijah found the sick people in the hut and remained with them, Efim had waited for his companion. First he went on a little way and sat down. There he waited and waited, dozed off, woke up again, and went on sitting—but no Elijah appeared. He looked and looked about for him, while the sun sank behind a tree—yet still no Elijah. "Can he have passed me," - thought Efim, - "or have been given a lift and so have driven past me, without noticing me where I sat asleep? Yet he could not have helped seeing me if that had been the case. In this steppe country one can see a long way. It would be no good my going back for him, since he might miss me on the road, and we should be worse off than ever. No, I win go on, and we shall probably meet at the next halting-place for the night." In time Efim came to a village, and asked the watchmen there to see to it that if such and such an old man (and he described Elijah) arrived later he should be directed to the same hut as himself. But Elijah never arrived to spend the night, so Efim went on again the next morning, asking everyone whom he saw if they had come across a baldheaded old man. No one had done so, however. Efim was surprised, but still pushed on alone. "We shall meet somewhere in Odessa," - he thought, - "or on board the ship," and forthwith dismissed the matter from his mind.

On the road he fell in with a pilgrim who, dressed in skull-cap and cassock, had been to Athos, and was now on his way to Jerusalem for the second time. They happened to lodge at the same place one night, and agreed henceforth to go together.

They arrived at Odessa without mishap, but were forced to wait three days for a ship. There were many other pilgrims waiting there, come from all parts of Russia, and among them Efim made further inquiries about Elijah, but no one had seen him.

The pilgrim told Efim how he could get a free passage if he wished, but Efim would not hear of it. "I would much rather pay," - he said. - "I have made provision for that." So he paid down forty roubles for a passage out and home, as well as laid in a stock of bread and herrings to eat on the way. In time the vessel was loaded and the pilgrims taken on board, Efim and the pilgrim keeping close to one another. Then the anchor was weighed, sail set, and they put out to sea. Ail that first day they had smooth sailing, but towards evening the wind arose, the rain came down, and the vessel began to roll heavily and ship water. The passengers were flung from side to side, the women began wailing, and those of the men whose stomachs were weaker than those of their fellows went below in search of berths. Efim too felt qualms, but repressed any outward manifestation of them, and remained sitting the whole of that night and the following day in the same position on deck which he had secured on embarking, and which he shared with some old people from Tamboff. They held on to their baggage, and squatted there in silence. On the third day it grew calmer, and on the fifth they put into Constantinople, where some of the pilgrims landed and went to look at the Cathedral of Saint Sophia, now a Mahomedan mosque. Efim did not land, but remained sitting where he was. After a stay of twenty-four hours they put to sea again, and, calling only at Smyrna and Alexandria, arrived without mishap at their port of destination, Jaffah. There all the pilgrims disembarked for the seventy kilometers tramp to Jerusalem, the business of landing being a nerve-shaking one for the poor people, since they had to be lowered into small boats, and, the ship's side being high and the boats rocking violently, it always looked as though the passenger would overshoot the boat. As a matter of fact, two men did get a ducking, but eventually everyone came safely to land. Once there, they lost no time in pushing forward, and on the fourth day arrived at Jerusalem. They passed through the city to a Russian hostel, showed their passports, had some food, and were conducted by the pilgrim around the Holy Places. To the actual Holy Sepulchre itself there was no admission that day, but they first of all attended Matins at the Greek Monastery of the Patriarch, where all pilgrims were gathered and placed men separate from women. They were told to take their shoes off and to sit around. A monk came out with a towel and started to wash everybody's feet; he washes, wipes and kisses, and that way he attended everyone. Wiped Efim's feet and kissed. They stood through vespers and matins, said their prayers and offered votive candles, handed in booklets inscribed with his parents' names. Here at the Patriarchate food and wine were given them. That first day also they were afforded a glimpse of the cell where Mary of Egypt took refuge, and duly offered candles there and recited a thanksgiving. Then they went on to the Monastery of Abraham in the Garden of Saveki, where Abraham once wished to sacrifice his son to the Lord. Thence they proceeded to the place where Christ appeared to Mary Magdalene, and thence to the Church of Saint James, the brother of Our Lord. At all these places the pilgrim acted as his guide, telling them everywhere how much to pay and where to offer candles. At length they returned to the hostel, and had just retired to rest when the pilgrim suddenly sprang up, and began rummaging among his clothes.

- Someone has stolen my purse and money! - He exclaimed. - The purse had twenty three roubles in it - two ten-rouble notes and three roubles in coin!

He raged and stormed for some time, but there was no help for it, and eventually they all lay down to sleep.

IX

Efim lay down with the rest, and a temptation fell upon him. "I do not believe," - he thought to himself, - "that the pilgrim was robbed, for he had nothing which thieves could take. He never gave anything anywhere. He told me to give, but never gave anything himself, and even borrowed a rouble of me."

But almost instantly he began to reproach himself for thinking so. "Who am I," - he said, - "to judge another? It is sinful of me, and I will refrain from these thoughts." It was not long, however, before he found himself remembering again how watchful of money the pilgrim had been, and how unlikely it was that his tale of being robbed could be true. - "He had nothing to be robbed of," - thought Efim once more. - "It was a mere excuse."

In the morning they rose and went to early mass at the great Church of the Resurrection—at the Holy Sepulchre itself. The pilgrim never left Efim, but walked by his side all the way.

When they entered the church they found a great crowd there, both of monks and pilgrims - Russian, Greek, Armenian, Turkish and Syrian, as well as of obscurer nationalities. Efim approached the Holy Gates with the others. A monk guided them. They passed the Turkish guards, and reached the spot where the Saviour was taken down from the Cross, and where now stood nine candlesticks with lighted tapers. There Efim offered a candle, and was then conducted by the monk up the steps on the right to Golgotha, to the spot where the Cross had stood. There Efim knelt down and prayed. Then he was shown the cleft where the earth was rent, the spot where Christ's hands and feet were nailed to the Cross, and the Tomb of Adam, where Christ's blood had trickled down upon Adam's bones. Next they came to the stone on which Christ sat while the Crown of Thorns was being placed upon His head, and then to the pillar to which He was bound for the scourging. Finally Efim saw the stone with the two holes for the feet of Christ. They would have shown him something more had not the crowd hurried forward, for all were eager to reach the actual catacomb of the Lord's Sepulchre. There a foreign Mass had just ended, and the Orthodox was beginning. Efim entered the Sepulchre with the rest.

He wanted to get rid of the pilgrim, for he found himself continually sinning in his thoughts against him; but the pilgrim still kept by his side, and entered with him into the Holy Sepulchre to hear Mass. They tried to get nearer to the front, but found it impossible, since the people were so closely packed that any movement either backward or forward was out of the question. As Efim stood gazing to the front and trying to pray, he found himself continually feeling for his purse. Two thoughts kept passing through his mind. The first was - "Is the monk cheating me all the time?" - and the second was - "If he has not been cheating me, and really had his purse stolen, why did they not do the same to me as well?"

X

As Efim stood thus, praying and gazing towards the chapel in which the actual Sepulchre stood, with thirty-six lamps always burning above it—suddenly, as he stood peering through the heads in front of him, he saw a strange thing. Immediately beneath the lamps, and ahead of all the congregation, he perceived an old man, dressed in a rough serge kaftan, and with a shining bald head like Elijah Bodroff's. "How exactly like Elijah he is!" - thought Efim to himself. "Yet it cannot possibly be he, for it would have been impossible for him to get here before myself. The last ship before our own sailed a whole week before we did, so he could never have caught it. And he certainly was not on our own, for I looked at every pilgrim on board."

Just as these thoughts had passed through Efim's mind, the old man in front began to pray, with three bows as he did so: one forwards, to God, and one on either side of him, to the whole Orthodox world. And lo! as the old man turned his head to bow towards his right, Efim recognized him beyond all possibility of doubt. It was Elijah Bodroff! Yes, that was Elijah's curly black beard—those were his eyebrows, his eyes, his nose—those were his features altogether! Yes, it was he, and nobody else—Elijah Bodroff!

Efim was overjoyed at having found his comrade, though also not a little surprised that Elijah could have arrived before him.

"He must have slipped past me somewhere, and then gone on ahead with someone who helped him on the way," - thought Efim. - "However, I will catch him as we pass out, and get rid of this pilgrim in the skull-cap. After that Elijah and I will keep together again. He might have got me to the front now if he had been with me."

So he kept his eyes fixed upon Elijah, determined not to lose sight of him. At last the Mass came to an end, and the people began to move. Indeed, there was such a crush as everyone pressed forward to kiss the Cross that Efim got jammed into a corner. Once more the thought that his purse might be stolen from him made him nervous, so he squeezed it tightly in his hand and set himself to force his way clear of the throng. Succeeding at last, he ran hither and thither, seeking Elijah, but eventually had to leave the church without having come across him. Next he visited the various hostels, to make inquiries about him, but, although he traversed the whole city, he could not find him anywhere. That evening, too, the pilgrim did not return. He had departed without repaying the rouble, and Efim was left alone.

Next day, Efim went to the Holy Sepulchre again, accompanied by one of the old men from Tamboff who had been with him on the ship. Once more he tried to get to the front, and once more he got thrust aside, so that he had to stand by a pillar to say his prayers. He peered through the heads in front of him again, and, behold! ahead of all the congregation, and under the very lamps of the Lord's Sepulchre, stood Elijah as before! He had his arms spread out like those of a priest at the altar, and his bald head was shining all over.

"Now," - thought Efim, - "I do not mean to lose him this time." So he started to worm his way forward, and eventually succeeded - but Elijah had vanished. He must have left the church.

The third day also Efim went to Mass, and once more looked for Elijah. And once more there stood Elijah, in the same position as before, and having the same appearance. His arms were spread out and he was gazing upwards, as though beholding something above him, while his bald head again shone brightly.

"Well," - thought Efim, - "come what may, I am not going to lose him this time. I will go straight away and post myself at the entrance, where we cannot possibly miss each other."

So he did so, and stood waiting and waiting as the people passed out; but Elijah did not come with them.

Efim remained six weeks in Jerusalem. He visited all the holy spots— Bethlehem, Bethany, the Jordan, and the rest—as well as had a new shirt stamped with a seal at the Holy Sepulchre (to be buried in one day), took away water from the Jordan in a phial, took away also earth and candles from the Holy Place, and spent all his money except just what was sufficient to bring him home again. Then he started to return, reached Jaffah, embarked, made the passage to Odessa, and set out upon his long overland tramp.

XI

Efim travelled alone, and by the same route as on the outward journey. Gradually as he drew nearer home there came back to him his old anxiety to know how things had been faring in his absence. "So much water passes down a river in a year!" - he thought. - "A home may take a lifetime to build up, and an hour to destroy." So he kept constantly wondering how his son had managed affairs since his departure, what sort of a spring it had been, how the cattle had stood the winter, and whether the new hut was finished.

When in time he arrived where he had parted from Elijah he found it hard to recognize the people of the locality. Where last year they had been destitute, to-day they were living comfortably, for the crops had been good everywhere. The inhabitants had recovered themselves, and quite forgotten their former tribulations. So it came about that one evening Efim was drawing near to the identical village where Elijah had left him a year ago. He had almost reached it, when a little girl in a white frock came dancing out of a hut near by, calling out as she did so:

- Grandfather! Dear grandfather! Come in and see us.

Efim was for going on, but she would not let him, and, catching him by the skirt of his coat, pulled him laughingly towards the hut.

Thereupon a woman and a little boy came out onto the steps, and the former beckoned to Efim, saying:

- Yes, pray come in, grandfather, and sup and spend the night.

So Efim approached the hut, thinking to himself, "I might get news of Elijah here, for surely this is the very hut to which he turned aside to get a drink."

He went in, and the woman relieved him of his wallet, gave him water to wash in, and made him sit down at the table; after which she produced milk, and dumplings, and porridge, and set them before him.

Efim thanked her kindly, and commended her readiness to welcome a pilgrim. The woman shook her head in deprecation of this.

- We could do no otherwise, - she answered, - for it was from a pilgrim that we learnt the true way of life. We had been living in forgetfulness of God, and He so punished us that we came very near to death's door. It was last year, in the summer, and things had gone so hard with us that we were, one and all, lying ill and starving. Of a surety we should have died, had not God sent to us just such another old man as yourself. He came in at midday, to beg a drink of water, and was seized with compassion when he saw us, and remained here. He gave us food and drink and set us on our feet, redeemed our land for us, bought us a horse and cart —and then disappeared.

The old woman entered the hut at this moment, and the younger one broke off.

- Yes, - went on the old woman, - to this day we do not know whether that man may not have been an angel of God. He loved us, pitied us, and yet went away without saying who he was, so that we know not for whom to pray. Even now it all passes before my eyes. I was lying there, waiting for death, when I chanced to look up and saw that an old man - an ordinary looking old man, except for his baldness - had entered to beg some water. I (may God forgive me for my sinfulness!) thought to myself: "Who is this vagabond?" Yet listen now to what he did. No sooner had he seen us than he took off his wallet, and, laying it down here - yes, here, on this very spot - unfastened it and...

- No, no, granny, - broke in the little girl, eagerly. - First of all he laid the wallet in the middle of the hut, and then set it on the bench.

And they fell to argue with one another in recalling Elijah's every word and deed - where he had sat, where he had slept, and all that he had said and done to everybody.

At nightfall the master of the house came riding up to the hut on horseback, and soon took up the tale of Elijah's life with them.

- Had he not come to us then, - he said, - we should all of us have died in sin; for, as we lay there dying and despairing, we were murmuring both against God and man. But this holy pilgrim set us on our feet once more, and taught us to trust in God and to believe in the goodness of our fellow men. Christ be with him! Before, we had lived only as beasts: it was he that made us human.

So these good people entertained Efim with food and drink, showed him to a bed, and themselves lay down to sleep. But Efim could not sleep, for the memory of Elijah - of Elijah as he had three times seen him at the head of the congregation in Jerusalem - would not leave him.

"Somewhere on the road he must have passed me," - he thought, - "Yet, however that may be, and no matter whether my pilgrimage be accepted or not, God has accepted him."

In the morning his hosts parted with Efim, loaded him with pasties for the journey, and went off to their work, while Efim pursued his way.

XII

Just a year had passed when Efim arrived home — arrived home in the spring. The time was evening, and his son was not in the hut, but at a tavern. At length he came home in drink, and Efim questioned him. There was abundant evidence that his son had been having a dissolute life in his absence. He had wasted all the money committed to his care, and neglected everything. His father broke out into reproaches, to which the son replied with insolence.

- You went gaily off on your travels, - he said, - and took most of the money with you. Yet now you require it of me!

The old man lost his temper and struck him.

Next morning, as he was going to the administrator to give up his passport, he passed Elijah's yard. On the lodge-step stood Elijah's old wife, who greeted Efim warmly.

- How are you, my good sir? - She said. - So you have returned safe and well?

Efim stopped.

- Yes, I have returned, glory be to God, - he replied. - But I lost sight of your good husband, although I hear that he is back now.

The old woman responded readily, for she loved chatting.

- Yes, he is back, good sir, - she said. - He returned some while ago - it was just after the Feast of the Assumption - and glad we were that God had brought him safely! We had been sadly dull without him. He can work but little now, for his best years lie behind him, but he remains always our head, and we are happier when he is here. How delighted our boy was! 'Life without daddy,' said he 'is like having no light to see by.' Yes, we found it dull indeed without Elijah. We love him too well not to have missed him sorely."

- Then perhaps he is at home at this moment?

- Yes, he is at home, and busy at his hive-bench, taking a swarm. He says that
the swarms have been magnificent this year—that God has given the bees
such health and vigour as he has never known before. Truly, he says, God is
not rewarding us according our sins. But come in, my dear sir. He will be
delighted to see you.

So Efim stepped through the lodge, crossed the courtyard, and went to find
Elijah in the bee-garden. As he entered it he caught sight of him - unprotected
by netting or gloves, and clad only in a grey jacket - standing under a young
birch tree. His arms were spread out and his face turned upwards, with the
crown of his bald head shining all over, as when he had stood those three
times by the Lord's Sepulchre in Jerusalem; while above him - as also in
Jerusalem - the sun was playing through the birch branches like a great
burning lamp, and around his head the golden bees were dancing in and out
and weaving themselves into a diadem, without stinging him. Efim stood still
where he was.

Then Elijah's wife called out:

- Here's your friend came to see you.

Elijah looked round, his face broke out into smiles, and he ran to meet his
comrade, gently brushing some bees from his beard as he did so.

- Good day to you, good day to you, my dear old friend! - He cried. - Then
did you get there safely?

- Yes, of a surety. My feet carried me safely, and I have brought you home
some Jordan water. Come and see me some time and get it. Yet I know not if
my task has been accepted of God, or...

- Surely, surely it has. Glory be to Him and to Our Lord Jesus Christ!

Efim went silent a moment, then continued:

- Yes, my feet carried me thither; but whether I was there also in spirit, or whether it were another who...

- Nay, nay. That is God's affair, my old comrade - God's affair.

- Well, on my way back, - added Efim, - I stopped at the hut where you parted from me.

Elijah seemed frightened, and hastened to interrupt him.

- That also is God's affair, my friend - God's affair, - he said. - But come into the hut, and I will get you some honey - and he hurried to change the conversation by talking of household matters.

Efim sighed, and quit reminding Elijah of the people in the hut or of his having seen him in Jerusalem.

And he understood: that in this world God has commanded everyone to work off his debt of duty by means of love and good works.